Cat-ographies

Persians
Long-Haired Friends

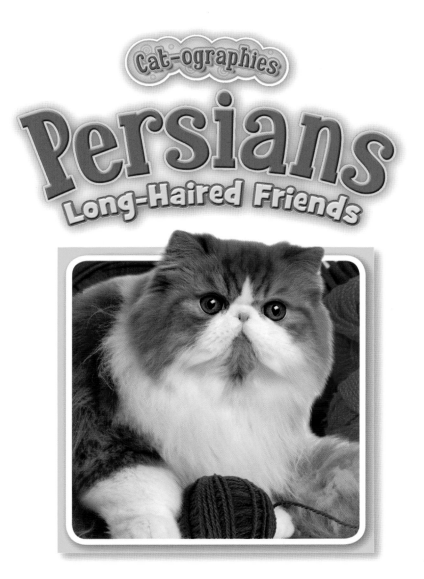

by Joyce Markovics

Consultant: Laura Matthews
Breeder, Persian & Exotic Shorthair Cats

BEARPORT
PUBLISHING

New York, New York

Credits

Cover and Title Page, © Eric Isselée/Shutterstock; TOC, © Medvedev Andrey/Shutterstock; 4, © Richard Katris/Chanan Photography; 5, © Richard Katris/Chanan Photography; 6, © Richard Katris/Chanan Photography; 7, Courtesy of The New York Public Library; 8L, © Maud D. Heaps/The Bridgeman Art Library/Getty Images; 8R, © Stock Montage/SuperStock; 9L, © Willard Culver/NGS Image Collection; 10T, © Frances M. Roberts/Newscom; 10B, © Emilio Ereza/Alamy; 11, © Linn Currie/Shutterstock; 12L, © Juniors Bildarchiv/Photolibrary; 12R, © cattyshackcreations/Solent News; 13TL, © Alan Robinson/Animal-Photography; 13TR, © Richard Katris/Chanan Photography; 13BL, © Jorg & Petra Wegner/Animals Animals Enterprises; 13BR, © Alan Robinson/Animal-Photography; 14L, © AP Images/Ed Bailey; 14R, © Lucas Jackson/Reuters/Landov; 15T, © Steve Gorton and Tim Ridley/Dorling Kindersley/Getty Images; 15B, Courtesy of William Yadlosky; 16, © Kim Kyung-hoon/Reuters/Landov; 17L, © Paulette Johnson/Fox Hill Photo; 17R, Courtesy of Dr. David Steele; 18, © Richard Katris/Chanan Photography; 19, © Paulette Johnson/Fox Hill Photo; 20, © NaturePL/SuperStock; 21, © Top-Pet-Pics/Alamy; 22, © Eric Isselée/Shutterstock; 23, © FotoJagodka/Shutterstock.

Publisher: Kenn Goin
Senior Editor: Lisa Wiseman
Creative Director: Spencer Brinker
Design: Dawn Beard Creative
Photo Researcher: Omni-Photo Communications, Inc.

Library of Congress Cataloging-in-Publication Data

Markovics, Joyce L.
  Persians : long-haired friends / by Joyce Markovics.
    p. cm. — (Cat-ographies)
  Includes bibliographical references and index.
  ISBN-13: 978-1-61772-141-0 (library binding)
  ISBN-10: 1-61772-141-7 (library binding)
  1. Persian cat—Juvenile literature. I. Title.
  SF449.P4M365 2011
  636.8'32—dc22
                    2010035155

For more information, write to Bearport Publishing Company, Inc., 101 Fifth Avenue, Suite 6R, New York, New York 10003. Printed in the United States of America in North Mankato, Minnesota.

113010
10810CGA

10 9 8 7 6 5 4 3 2 1

Contents

Top Puffball

Meows and cheers filled the 2009 International Cat Show in Atlanta, Georgia. More than 600 cats were **competing** for the top prize—**Best in Show**. A black Persian (PUR-zhun) cat named Gorilla gazed at the crowd with his shining copper-colored eyes. He was among the youngest and fluffiest of the competitors.

Gorilla's full name is Kuorii Gorilla of Cuzzoe, but his owners affectionately call him "Gorilla," or "Go-Go" for short.

The judges carefully examined all the cats, including Gorilla. Each animal was a great example of its **breed**, but the judges had to pick a favorite. After much discussion, they finally made a decision. One judge held up the winning cat. The crowd went wild. Gorilla had won!

Gorilla is shown here after winning Best in Show at the International Cat Show—the biggest cat show in the United States. Each year it is held in a different city, such as Atlanta, or "Catlanta" as cat lovers call it.

According to **The Cat Fanciers' Association**, Persians are the most popular cat breed in the world.

Cats of Persia

Gorilla is not only a champ, but he's also a wonderful pet. "He follows us around like a puppy, and he loves to climb up in our laps," said his proud owners, Justin Pelletier and Eric Valencia. The loving relationship that Gorilla has with his owners is typical of a Persian. The special **bond** between these cats and humans dates back hundreds of years.

Gorilla poses with his owners, Eric Valencia (left) and Justin Pelletier (right), and breeder Paolo Carnevaletti (middle).

In fact, Persians are one of the oldest cat breeds. They were first raised in Persia, which is now the country of Iran. The cats were prized for their long, soft fur. An Italian explorer, Pietro della Valle (1586–1652), is believed to have discovered these long-haired cats during a trip to Persia. He thought the cats were beautiful and decided to bring some back to Europe with him in 1620.

Where Persian Cats Came From

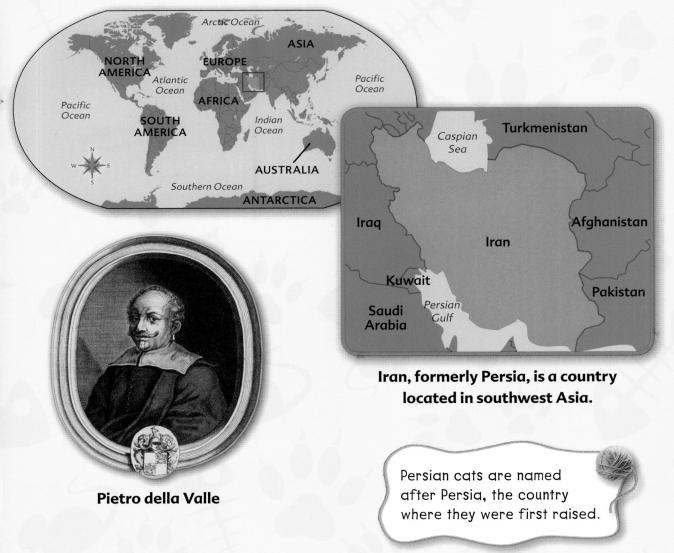

Iran, formerly Persia, is a country located in southwest Asia.

Pietro della Valle

Persian cats are named after Persia, the country where they were first raised.

Love at First Meow

In Europe, these long-haired cats soon became a favorite among **royalty**. Not only were the cats beautiful, they made great **companions** because they were sweet, **loyal**, and very calm. Queen Victoria of England (1819–1901) kept two grayish-blue Persians as cuddly pets.

The Persians that lived in Europe hundreds of years ago looked similar to this cat.

Queen Victoria of England

In the 1800s, Americans traveling to Europe also fell in love with these cats and took them home. The breed soon became a hit in the United States. These early Persians looked different than they do today. They were larger and had bigger **muzzles**. Over time, the cats were **bred** to be smaller, between 7 and 12 pounds (3 and 5 kg), and to have the round, flat, pushed-in faces they are now known for.

By the 1900s, Persians were very popular pets in America.

The famous English nurse, Florence Nightingale (1820–1910), kept many Persian cats as pets. Her favorite was a large male named Mr. Bismark.

9

Pansy Face

The Persian's flat face is one of its most unique **traits** and sets it apart from other breeds. Many people think the shape of its face looks like a **pansy**—a type of flower that is round and flat.

A pansy

The Persian's face is flat like a pansy.

Persians are considered to be medium-size cats. They have **stout** legs, round paws, and a very furry tail. Persians also have huge, round eyes. Centered between their large eyes is a tiny nose. All these features give Persians what people call a sweet expression.

While most Persians, such as this one, have copper-colored eyes, some have blue or green eyes.

Persians love to rub and press their flat faces against their human companions. This is known as "rubbing up" and is a sign of affection.

Persians also look different from other types of cats because they have long **coats**—the longest of any breed. Most cats have fur that doesn't grow longer than about four inches (10 cm). However, the Persian's coat can grow up to eight inches (20 cm) long! Persians have two layers of fur—a short **undercoat** and a longer outercoat. Their fur is soft, silky, and thick enough to keep them warm in cold weather.

A Persian's long, fluffy fur makes the cat look a lot larger than it actually is.

Danelle German's cat-fur handbags

A cat **groomer** named Danelle German turns the fur that she trims from Persian cats into yarn. She then uses the yarn to knit cat-fur handbags!

Persians come in a wide range of colors such as silver, gold, red, blue, or black. The most popular color, however, is white. These cats also come in different patterns such as **tabby** and **tortoiseshell**.

A gold Persian

A tabby Persian

A blue Persian

A tortoiseshell Persian

Groom Time

Like other cats, Persians lick their fur to keep it clean. However, a Persian's long, flowing coat needs extra care. The fur tangles and easily becomes **matted**. To avoid this, a Persian must be brushed or combed every day and bathed about every six weeks.

Some owners give their Persians special "lion trims." This means the cat's body is shaved, except for its head, legs, and the tip of its tail, making it look like a little lion. This kind of trim keeps the cat cool and knot-free.

A Persian with a lion trim

A Persian being combed

Betty Yadlosky, a cat breeder, knows all about taking care of cats with long fur. She has 11 Persians! Each one needs to be regularly groomed, especially the cats that compete in shows. It can take Betty up to two hours to wash and blow-dry a single cat.

This Persian is having its fur dried with a blow-dryer.

Betty Yadlosky, her great-granddaughter Sophia, and one of Betty's Persians at a show

Cat Care

In addition to grooming their pets, owners also need to take care of their cats by bringing them to a **veterinarian** each year. The vet can check the animals for diseases and other health issues, such as breathing problems. Sadly, up to 40 percent of Persian cats get **kidney disease**.

Some Persians have eye problems and breathing issues due to their flat faces, so it's important for owners to take their pets to a vet every year.

To keep Persians safe from being attacked by other animals or getting hit by a car, breeders recommend keeping them inside at all times. Being outside could also cause their heavy fur to become matted or they could **overheat** in hot weather.

During a visit to the vet, owners should also have their pets' teeth checked. Some Persians have **abnormal** teeth. This can cause many problems, such as making it hard for them to chew food. One cat born with abnormal teeth is Sebastian, a black Persian from Indiana. His two bottom teeth stick out of his mouth. His owner, dentist David Steele, protects Sebastian's fangs from breaking by covering them with gold **crowns**!

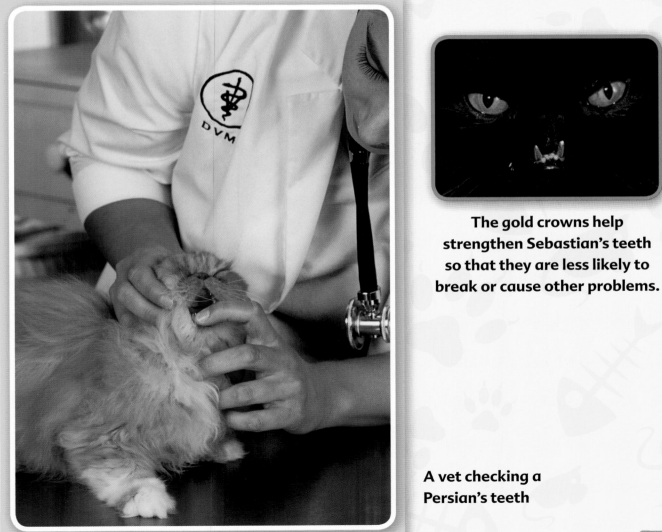

The gold crowns help strengthen Sebastian's teeth so that they are less likely to break or cause other problems.

A vet checking a Persian's teeth

Mothers and Kittens

Owners need to take special care of female Persians that are going to have kittens. Females that are ready to give birth require a quiet, safe place to have their kittens. Although mother cats can have up to 15 kittens at a time, they usually have only 3 to 5.

Because Persian cats are so sweet and loving, they make great mothers.

Persian kittens are born with lots of fur and with their eyes closed. They feed on their mother's milk for up to six weeks. By the time they are eight weeks or a little older, Persian kittens are able to leave their mother. Then they can go live with a loving human family.

A mother Persian feeding her kittens

After they are born, it takes 10 to 14 days for Persian kittens to open their eyes.

Lounge Lizards

While Persian kittens are very playful, adult cats are very calm. They are sometimes called "**lounge lizards**" because they enjoy just lying around. A Persian's favorite place is a comfy couch or chair or someone's lap. People who want a very active cat should consider other breeds, such as the Siamese.

Persians love to drape themselves over furniture. They often blend right in.

With proper care, a Persian can live to be 15 to 20 years old.

Persians love to be petted and fussed over for hours. Their mild and easygoing manner allows them to get along with everyone—other cats, dogs, and especially children. For many owners, these puffballs are the perfect pets!

Persians enjoy the company of people and other animals, like this Labrador retriever.

Persians at a Glance

Weight:	Between 7 and 12 pounds (3 and 5 kg)
Height at Shoulder:	About 10–15 inches (25–38 cm)
Coat Hair:	Long, thick, and silky
Colors:	They come in many colors such as white, silver, gold, red, blue, and black. They can also come in patterns such as tabby and tortoiseshell.
Country of Origin:	Persia (modern-day Iran)
Life Span:	15 to 20 years
Personality:	Affectionate, sweet, and laid-back; love people; not very active
Special Physical Characteristics:	Long fluffy coat; large, round head; flat face; big eyes; small nose; and a broad body with stout legs

Glossary

abnormal (ab-NOR-muhl) unusual or not normal

Best in Show (BEST IN SHOH) the top-rated cat in a cat show

bond (BOND) a close, emotional connection

bred (BRED) mated cats from specific breeds to produce young with certain characteristics

breed (BREED) a kind of cat

Cat Fanciers' Association, The (KAT FAN-see-urz uh-*soh*-see-AY-shuhn, THUH) an organization that keeps records on different cat breeds

coats (KOHTS) the fur or hair on cats or other animals

companions (kuhm-PAN-yuhnz) animals or people who spend time with someone

competing (kuhm-PEET-ing) taking part in a contest

crowns (KROUNZ) metal or porcelain caps placed on teeth

groomer (GROOM-ur) a person who washes, combs, and cares for animals

kidney disease (KID-nee duh-ZEEZ) an illness that can cause a person or animal's kidneys, which are body parts that remove waste, to stop working

lounge lizards (LOUNJ LIZ-urdz) animals or people who like to lie in a lazy or relaxed manner

loyal (LOI-uhl) faithful to others

matted (MAT-id) badly tangled fur or hair

muzzles (MUHZ-uhlz) the noses, mouths, and jaws of some kinds of animals, such as cats and dogs

overheat (*oh*-vur-HEET) to become too hot

pansy (PAN-zee) a round, flat garden flower

royalty (ROI-uhl-tee) kings, queens, princes, and princesses

stout (STOUT) strong and sturdy

tabby (TAB-ee) having fur with a striped pattern

tortoiseshell (TOR-tuhss-*shell*) having a coat that has markings like those found on a tortoise's shell

traits (TRAYTS) qualities or characteristics of someone or something

undercoat (*uhn*-dur-KOHT) the short, soft layer of fur on an animal's body

veterinarian (*vet*-ur-uh-NER-ee-uhn) a doctor who cares for animals

Index

Bibliography

Müller, Ulrike, and Colleen Power. *Persian Cats: A Complete Pet Owner's Manual.* Hauppauge, NY: Barron's Educational Series (2004).

animal.discovery.com/breedselector/catprofile.do?id=3080

www.cfainc.org/breeds/profiles/persian.html

www.tica.org

Read More

Crisp, Marty. *Everything Cat: What Kids Really Want to Know About Cats.* Chanhassen, MN: NorthWord Press (2003).

Perkins, Wendy. *Persian Cats.* Mankato, MN: Capstone Press (2008).

Learn More Online

To learn more about Persians, visit
www.bearportpublishing.com/Cat-ographies

About the Author

Joyce Markovics is an editor, writer, and orchid collector. She lives with her husband, Adam, who is allergic to furry animals, and their pet land crab, Dirk.